Duality Lies Beneath

Poems

Josh Dale

ISBN-13: 978-0692709733
Cover design by Josh Dale
Printed in the U.S.A.

For more titles and inquiries, please visit:
www.thirtywestph.com

Contents

A foolish consistency is the hobgoblin of little minds, adored by little statesmen and philosophers and divines. With consistency a great soul has simply nothing to do. He may as well concern himself with his shadow on the wall.

—Ralph Waldo Emerson, *Self-Reliance*

Duality Lies Beneath

Theory of Birth

A baby's skin reacts to oxygen
for the first time,
the cavity calls for us
identity feelings vibrations senses.
No idea what is happening.

Sight is an unfathomable murk.
Smell is a repugnant waft.
Touch is an intimidating umbilical cord.
Taste is an apprehensive placenta.
The rich, the genius, the criminal
all hung by the ankle like a
slab of sirloin for salivating mother.

We unclose our eyes
from a natal bliss,
take optical notes before us
of muck and steel
the alien and unreal.

It is with
fluid-filled lungs
we scream
like the Ouroboros on its
final portion.

Natural?

I never feel the need to catalog
because Whitman did it for me.
Grab the hilt and walk with me,
And don't apologize,
empathize.
You're dying too.
Everything has been through me,
Fucked up and contrived into me.

I don't deal in absolutes
but I advise you to stay
off the Astroturf.
The plush isn't authentic,
It is not Whitmanian.
It does not breathe our air,
but exhales the scent of deceit
and a multitude of chemicals.

Feed

With the hoe at our feet,
we wipe a day's work away
and watch the supply trucks
drive off into the sunset.
We gorge the growth of tomorrow
in minute bites all our lives.

My continual growth
is for me and me only.
Me, mine, always for myself.
Corn.
Corn.
Even more corn!
Fabulous.
Fucking.
Food.

But it's not worth bemoaning.
The scythe will arrive
and take it all away.

Waste

Food is food unless your
gut says otherwise
If food is in your belly,
you'll keep eating, and hoarding.
The instinct when you're famished

Food isn't free
but it roams all around us
It is placed on shelves
until it is placed
in the dumpster.
Then it is spoiled

You may wonder what Neanderthals
did with their uneaten game.
Chasing dreams and death,
spoiling the anticipation
of drawing first blood
over a crude campfire

To the Ferraro Rocher Box in the Trash

You protrude a diagonal diamond
in a circle hole of eternity plastic
Orion's Belt is the same overhead
as it was since its death erupted
the cold gust on my face
gasoline filling tank
sheering off more fossils by the ml
tearing up my eyes
artic howl as if
I was missing a variable
that included your name in my phone
in full because I'm that type of person
to insert your government name, not a nickname.

Yes, sir, I *am* crying, ok? Please let me be
to watch the stupid gas pump tv station
thing in peace. Look, Jimmy Kimmel is speaking to me
and me alone. He keeps calling for
me but only in the 2nd person. So, maybe
when I'm done, I'll be rude and walk inside
and buy a 3-pk Ferraro Rocher and proceed to
split it three ways: one for me, one for Jimmy,
and one for you,
the trashcan, of course.

Coffee from Ethiopia & A Plum from Chile

I'll never see the calloused-handed farmers or the rusty barge that brought these arabica beans and stone fruits to my hands. But I do feel the sizzling until it's over. It's just a curdled husk dumped into a plastic trash bag. I'll enjoy the essence from the enticing cup and bite into the flesh that drips onto my chin before I wipe it off my lips with a paper towel and throw that into the plastic trash bag, too. It's only enjoyed once; the first time. And then it's repeated innocuously the next day and the next day, and it becomes a habit and the next day, and we can be here all day. Unless you go broke, theft is always an option. Raid those crates in the prep room at first, then seize those cargo ships at the port of entry.

Just Plain Vanilla

Vanilla cake and ice cream
is an American staple like
white bread and milk
before a blizzard
the dinner table is set
bucolic rust calls for most of us
the dollar double cheeseburger
that tastes of ammonia
no frills all classic
mostly for the dying age
that held down the fort
and fucked around enough
for us in the future to find out
their follies so that's why we're enraged
but crucifixion looks like
it fucks sucks hence why
we stopped hanging
and firing squads
and guillotines
when you mix vanilla and chocolate
and strawberry you become a mess
but a tasty mess that doesn't
exactly taste like anything you
can point a finger at but
it's not like I'm the only one
indulging in chaos

Inflammatory

The acquisition of paychecks
doesn't pay for life anymore
maybe for the silent observers or
standard issue warriors
that put down hungry dogs
before they breed

Allocations of food and sunlight
ergonomics and machinations
only for the good guys that
came home and changed it all

Write your dreams and hopes
on pieces of paper
and burn them away
watch the ashes flutter
and go off to distant parts

You did the hard work early
they don't tell you
it all burns in the end
it all rots in the end

Green Light Catastrophe

Obscurity in motion
behind hazy blue curtains
with a trickle of liquid
bitter like molten forge water
at the bottom of a barrel
of a gun
Metal-on-metal bashing
screeching rubber dying by the millimeter
running vigilant lights that police
the people
A slurring of better judgment
aiming inanimate steel
descended from Gaston Glock's workbench
grasped in white-knuckle fury
Little else is known or heard
since the echo bounces off sturdy facades
only rings once.

Haikus

1

The flowers have bloomed
and the locusts devour
any sign of life.

2

Oily dressing with
the pit-marked spinach leaves on
my baby-blue plate.

3

A doe has died on
the searing blacktop. It still
continues to smile.

4

My gaze, downward, with
all the plastic faces here.
Coffee stains shirt brown.

7

Fluttering bird speaks
your name only once per day
choking on the seed.

8

Please and thanks and a
firm handshake is how killers
pay the bills these days.

Prayer for Static

the sky is orange for once
as I write this
praying for grey-backed clouds
to morph failures and
plummet onto bitter tongues
and speak to you and
you and every atom in between
fissuring and conjoining
simultaneously

somewhere else a siren call
for a broken finger or the last ride
out at 8:43 PM
time of death
awaits no one these days
yet sky is still orange
and sublime and joyous
like it's always been
since we knew what the
sky was

finally a breeze
kisses unwarranted grime
off face of indifference
will it still be here like
the laws dictate
like the prophecy foretold

there's a chance it will come
without us knowing
or it'll burn a slow coal fire
shoot geysers from legs
fractured and decayed
not like we're using them

I replace the headphones on
and tap a pitiable foot
until that siren blends
static to tissue
to rain and grey
for once it is not orange

Rats and Roaches

After the Swift shower
and all the asphalt dries and cures
and ivory towers resettle
do we find the exposé?
creatures from the night
crying wolf with a
skinned sheep mask
dripping fresh blood

Obelisks downtown
where all the monies are
congregated bliss
above the pigeon shit
and woes of man
where clouds go to drink and
spit into a godly mouth

Beneath corporate refuse
and the bottom line
the rats and roaches lie
in wait for their savior's scraps
recesses in the
exhumation thrive in
the humid musk

Not every boot tramples

most scurry away

just like the rats and roaches

no one wants to see them

no one wants to be touched by them

unless they swarm

Upon the Mantle

that kid in the ornate oval
marred by oxidation and time
upon the granite mantle

> was once the angel, the sweet aphorism
> the one that'll make it and change the world
> upon the proud family's mantle

sepia-toned eyes, burned at the corners
a stoic daguerreotype
upon that decrepit mantle

> it's so still and weathered
> for all to see
> for all to forget

A Prison of Rain

Cloudy rains keep me inside
a pavilion is a prison when
rain drops from shingle like bars
plod though mud
the grey outstretched a tight
canvas over treetops
sludge metal drowns your eardrums
but on the other side birds rejoice
and dance inside the wind currents
as the drops slam your face it feels
like a steady compress of needles
evenly distributed to support
the weight of your wrinkles

#94

Staring at the window
after a stormy day
and seeing the accumulated
rain drops trickle down.
Each drop: a tear, a memory
of celestial beings, poisoned
by noxious fumes.
Some run fast;
the wax of life.
Some remain still
and accumulate rainbows.

Some days, I just want to shout at the rain,
to tell them—those heavenly deities—
everything will be alright;
purged and washed away.

And You'd Believe It

we build walls to keep marauders out
just look at the Vatican the Chinese et al
but these days we build long roads
for white flight to escape
to then absorb, eventually
but they bitch when the steel mills close
say it's the end of America's greatness
and scapegoats are sheared
to the bone
but the money goes and
the money stays as long as the
realtors predict more snow
fewer potholes in that turn of the century
row home you think is chic because
of the shutters and the value
keeps on going up cause Ben Franklin
pissed on the cornerstone in 1781
another vicious cycle that
descendants will study one day
looking out of the window bored
at the colossus that we built
on backs tooth and nail
building walls to keep us in
the tubes, now plaque-infested
keep you right where they want you

What a legacy means

I remember the day Tom Petty died the
first thing I did was load up Wikipedia
instead of blasting "Won't Back Down"
in my office because the only way to
know someone is truly gone these days
is to wait for their Wikipedia to go from
'is' to 'was' and I wish I had a fanatical
blinking spell or that feeling of being punched
in the gut or anything like that.
Yes, he was a great man but I've only
known of his voice and his hands
and not his vices and demons while he
didn't even know I existed. I imagine at some
point he would've just insinuated that the millions
of fans throughout the years exist or else he
would've gone broke so there's the unseen benefit
there despite me not having a name but a number.
They say never meet your heroes because they
will only disappoint you and I can see why
because you spend countless hours performing
mental charades of the day you were to meet them
and wearing out the special hat or a vinyl record
passed down from your parents or how you'd
feel that butterfly fluttering in your gut moments
before they lay their eyes on you and say:

Hi, uh, what's your name? Cool, man, nice to meet you.
I hereby acknowledge you exist, and I am
appreciative of sharing a space of oxygen
and other carcinogens with you for the 30 seconds
I have to allocate per fan which is then multiplied
by 150—since that's how many backstage VIP packages
were sold—and there we go again. I just quantified you
as a number and I apologize again but here, this
signed tour t-shirt will be worth a couple grand
once I perish so don't wash it out, ok?

And then he's onto shaking another hand,
spreading another germ while you are left
with a relic, a legacy of a waning era of freedom,
of prowess, of opportunity that only comes
around once ever and then you take your seat and
guzzle a beer before the show and embrace the
time that "I saw Tom Petty" goes from 'is' to 'was,'
when you, ultimately, join the past tense and
never look back again cause the past doesn't
create new things and knowing that we will
never see the 27-Club age a day older really
hits you in the gut but it's probably better that
way because youth is what we all have at one time
so, buy that ticket, see that hero, don't edit
Wikipedia to resurrect the dead because
there's probably a Valhalla for us all and it
isn't worth mentally preparing for the
'was' just yet.

All Sewer Drains Smell the Same

All sewer drains smell the same,

no matter which rank city.

They say the ancient Greeks

invented indoor plumbing,

but they never thought it would

end up like this.

There is a slight change in

the biochemistry of the bowel,

whether you're in New York or New Delhi,

Los Angeles or London,

Barcelona or Beijing.

But the compost builds

exponentially and overflows.

It's hard to circumnavigate it all

so, we just stay in one place.

One synthetic being of

diversified shit, and even when

the temporary rain dissolves us,

there're carbon monoxide molecules

dying and making it all worse.

A Dogpile of Refuse

The department store is the
smelting pot of corporate refuse
I imagine an assembly line,
the rivets, the metallic taste
in my mouth, every rotating shift
I exit with lead in my stomach.

This is where all the artists go
to die, encased in their polymer
shells and wrapped in plastic film
both are made from dinosaurs and sullied
with face-value stickers, it's a
dogpile, reciprocity of refuse,
dust collecting on immortality in
both theory and function.

Scream from the bottom and
suck air through straws the
bargain bins experience turnover
and it's the pressure that kills.

I sit in the same ice chest

I sit in the same ice chest
with the same long face
and raccoon'd eyes,
breathing through my nose
with the off chance, I open
my mouth to gasp.

I see the same powerline,
the same traffic jam,
the same birds shitting on the window,
the same landscapers working through
rain, wind, and sunshine,
wishing they'd open the window to
let me breathe.

I screen the same call from The Man
about the same project on a different border,
ever wondering if my computer
laughs when I go upstairs.

Recently, we all got messenger bags
and a hard hat.
He joked we should make it dirty first
or else they'll make fun of you.
I spit on it and let it be.

There's a hole in my ice chest
it lets all the heat in.
I don't care about it anymore.

The Eave of Something Different

I swear there's a love story in here
just need to make it through the night
sweat drops on the bed sheet
that hold their form for a few
seconds and then collapse
the a/c is on but the clothes aren't
cooling down fast enough but I fell
asleep in these Lee jeans and hands
cross across my chest as I lay dying
exhuming a corpse in hell
bukowski quotes are popping
into my synapses but there's too many
living poems standing on my bookshelf
like rowlock bricks that need to be read
first and foremost why am I still sweating
one eve before my birth knelt over
like a genuflecting priest by the pew but
carpet plush is what makes the bed warmer
at night than a summer's dream laced
with sleep apnea and asphyxiation nightmares
I should get that checked but first a nap
after work and a forgotten phone call
after forgotten phone call later and it's winter
where I loathe the ground I walk on and
I'm clawing at my neck like a
gregor samsa caricature that was
born a day before me why can't I share
the room in which you wrote so I think
about the powerade in the fridge but here
I kneel as a monk in shangri-la
body bending floor joists I sort my laundry
sip the water from the holy grail that's plastic
I do not complain but think of rest and
gratitude knowing that someone must open
the park down the road at dawn and promptly
close it at dusk now if that's not dedication
I might as well be dead

Midnight

The inception of one.

The cessation of another.

The moment where time does not—

And cannot—exist,

For it is but a human contraption,

Built to cleave a rift in an on-going

Tug of the ethereal tether,

Binding us all to the masthead

Of reality.

What is reality to the acorn,

Complacent and humble,

Upon the grassy, mirrored hedge?

What is the elliptical to the spherical?

When perceived plains are flat?

It takes a trained eye to observe the phases

Of the moon,

Of the luminous deity waxing and waning

With every mechanical stroke of the watch hands.

A click, and then a pause, vacuumed-sealed air,

Unpermitted to touch beating breath.

A sliver of Einstein's brain is hermetically

divided between two museums

Yet the tired eye unravels dust upon the dawn.

The answer lies in grey.

The hollow-bearing of a life lost in shadow's hue.

Denizens of Gaia, bloodshot and malicious,

Piss away the daily sin at midnight's end.

Dirty Bathroom Mirror

is still there to reflect all your

red-eyed early morning scowls

accentuate the bags under the eyes

observes toothpaste spittle on your chin

the more vigorous you brush

the more that gets on the mirror

until it's blotted out white creamy

paste all forlorn gazes

and subcutaneous fat pinches

and all those times you raised a fist to

the reason looking back daring to

seize through and grab it by the neck

and never let go until it breaks

splinters and cracks on fertile flesh

blood oozing like geyser dormant

a sight for swords as eyes

always jabbing at what can't speak

Drains

I look down into the muck

of my bathroom sink,

listen to the satisfying sizzle

of hydrogen peroxide.

Where do sewers go for a baptism?

Charon knows the drill.

My toilet does, too.

A lot of what I've said before

is as mundane as this atomical process.

I can hear the atoms fizzle.

I can hear my atoms fizzling,

separating right

into two.

This Poem is About Triangles

This poem is about triangles
and how many points can taper into infinity
whilst disregarding the hypotenuse of incongruence.
                         (hypothesis) (ignorance)
There is a certain degree to which one can imagine
the ancient Egyptians shoved stones
down the mouth of the Nile
via inclined planes,
(which are triangles by association)
thus damming the flood.
Reaching infinity at the apex
while buzzards swarm the locust buzz.
Think of how insolent a triangle is
when it involves three lovers
with three separate angles
on a single circle of lust.
3   6   0
as we revolve around this round world
and remain in the same spot
as obtuse asteroids barrel past
the sundial of Pythagoras—broken.

Poems of a Maze

The sunken nail splinters
wood and to be
removed slides out whole
allowing the wood to bleed

I am the plank forever
imbued with nail
iron zinc and other
heavy metals that don't
expunge when lungs
inflate and then
flatten

as if the stigmata don't
already burn with lead
the exit to the maze
fades into a wall
where I am pinned to
in the end

***

I drive my car into a telephone pole
as a way to circumvent the maze
of substance abuse
for time and space waits for
no trivial human qualms
and they drop the charge of
driving without a seatbelt
as if it's a blessing to me

***

It's not like we matter when the
shareholders meet around the
greedy table discussing matters
that we can't comprehend
and dictate who gets paid what
and how far up the bottom line
goes while we stand in awe with
a pole ready to snap beneath
exasperated torsos and legs that
cannot stand without a crutch
eyes that cannot shed
another tear

A Dirge at My Door

A dirge at my door rings ears, scratches head, nods
like ghosts of a black wedding outweighing light

It looks like rain today, so stay outside with
your wet feet, trembling

In the pit of my chest, my heart thumping slow,
like a death race to the end of the line

Vice grips on my temple, restricting flow, turning malignant
it's hard to smile right anymore
it's hard to breathe right anymore
it's hard to think right anymore
it is hard
to be
right

To keep me from fracturing, grab me by
both shoulders and shake me back
to reality and let me hear it from
the bastard's mouth:

Everything is going fine
do not worry
so much

I don't think the dirge will cease
I don't see it coming to look for me

This thing

This thing called Peace

The email that finds you well

is lost amongst 999+ other emails that have found you with blurry incoherent eyes scanning and doomscrolling and popping notification pills with your Zoloft and crummy tap water. And then the ones that find you unwell are always the ones you happen to skim across when you're already in the gutter and unlike Oscar Wilde, you're not looking up at the stars but a blue-light rectangle containing anything and everything turned to the highest brightness exactly 5'-9.5" away from an airport outlet as you wait for the snow to calm the fuck down and the tarmac to turn black again. It's time to leave it all behind the email says to you buried under other emails all hoping to find you well. And just like the snow burying you and thousands of others it's time to leave it all behind.

Blown Pixie Dust

Silver and Gold
They say are precious metals
but I am titanium
horizontally intact
and this velvet pavement:
guacamole on a blue-marbled plate.
You know how Plato points up
and Aristotle forward?
Like Gods we reach out.
Like Gods do we advocate.
As do the dust of cosmic ancients:
Breath in.
Pixie dust out.
We're magic, you know?
But our vices make us mundane.
My undercarriage
is riddled with rust
as my mind inhales
my lot of pixie dust
I should feel privileged I'm not dead.

Detachment

Begone timesheets!

Crumpled and tossed into static blue.

We are all semi-trucks

semi-apportioned,

loads continue to mature and fill.

We guzzle gallons of stress down life's freeway,

some blow a tire, others a head gasket.

We wish to seize stones lodged in tire treads,

and throw them continentally.

Detachment begins at the chain's end

until the California coast is in sight.

Never to oil, but rust,

become a slave to nature.

Gauges glazed over and cracked,

we are reclaimed in time,

oxidized until the chassis snaps

with just a bird's perching.

Every 3,000 Miles

The downpours arrive today drowning in cherry blossoms deep within the puddles impossible to count droplets pints and gallons amalgam a car plows through it like a sword cleaving a sea pour it all onto your head and watch it leave a crisp sheen like you're right off the assembly line and you are the new owner sign here here and here if you'd like the extended warranty but remember you're given 3,000 miles until you warrant some sort of maintenance and if you let your hands off the wheel the tires will guide you based on the direction of previous drivers that have worn down the asphalt millimeter by millimeter but wait whoa watch out you're about to veer off into the collapse shoulder like you tore a rotator cuff tackling the stud running back pry your sorry ass with the jaws of life crumpled fender and all recalls considered they will strap your down and slam the door and skedaddle off to hospital x and as the ambulance wails your siren song a tire will plunge into the same cherry blossom pothole and send sparkles into the air like firecrackers

Thirty-eight cents

I found thirty-eight cents in your purse today.

When 1999 was brand new.

Grocery and department stores now

defunct; unspent,

your library card remains

unused; pristine.

I want to check out the books you've read,

learn more about the parting soul.

University of Penn contact cards, too.

I should call to see if they still

practice transplanting livers.

I know the surgeon is dead by now.

Lipstick, Wintergreen gum, mascara,

calculator, peach pralines, pictures.

Many pictures,

of me and others,

but mostly me.

Tissue with your germ,

how I blow my nose and dry my eyes

with(out) you here.

With(in) me.

The Wax has Run Dry

this window isn't
what it used to be
as you water the poinsettia
the soil bubbles with something
called life and it smells
like decay
there is a draft coming in
defying entropy tingling
the hand you once held
it's blue now so blue
you'd think it conquered the sky
you'd think it exhumed the worms
yet here we are
in wake of winter
looking for something to
affix the eyes
the shroud is dense
and it is finite
and it will turn to dust
when you allow it
to finally dry out
on the mantle
as your prized heirloom
a trophy of past battles won
and the glory days
only you both know
the rain

running paint

expediting the inevitable

the rust that flakes

the mold that grows

in the darkest corners

is the hardest to kill

cough a part of yourself

out into the wild

the unfamiliar

it isn't up to you anymore

the wax has run dry

glazing over the pain

enough to squeeze

and exhale

the life from your eyes

into wall

into stone

into nothing at all

Carve

Between two voids there is a mountain
you must carve through
under any circumstance are you to
stop unless you
stop breathing
towering overhead, it laughs
rain on your forehead
when you slow down the
bugs crawl and buzz around you
your blood is more valuable to them
than your weary muscles

The mountain asks you
which creature is more agile
the bird in the air
or the fish in ocean
and as you pick away
you're getting to the point
of failure and you wish to pause
but the mountain scolds you
and you persevere through spite

You can't gauge your strength
but you endeavor onward and the
byproduct of your digging creates
more mountains behind you and
eventually, you reach the other side
but it isn't what you expect and thus
the void draws you in like a vacuum

Maybe the mountain isn't benevolent
or diabolical in the slightest
it just is the mountain in which you carve
so, if you stop you just lay supine and ask
how many raindrops must fall
on my upturned face
to be classified as tears

What Comes Next

the war is over
and the good guys came home
to spread uniforms among
the acres of fertile
plush they called a home

Levittown being Patient X
in this charade of progress
rows and rows split
by asphalt and sod
you'd think this is how prison is made

then the architects came without
a warrant but did it anyway
refacing decades-old facades
and bombed-out steel mills
change with the times
slinging architectural jargon
up with the cranes
appeasing land developers

sorry grandad your life was full of stress and COPD
and I was a naughty grandson
but that one fishing trip was enough
and I remember the hook in my shirt
time to time and laugh
thinking how blue the sky was
and the water it reflected

hope you like what you see
I hold the prototypes in rolls
and how often do I want them
piled into a pyre and lit up

All Flags, Above All Men

all flags, above all men hang it horizontal

at peace and war

cold and bare it weeps

for it cannot escape the beating sun

taste the wind and the rain morphed into a pulp

it weeps again

god particles where it stands

something besides me, flown to nothing

into the mystery

it is gone

it is gone.

Gathering of Shadows

A swirling drain hole of black,
taking everything down the goo of my innards.
Viscous bile covering, sticking to my hands.
A sloppy murk is what my heart has become.
Sickly and liquefied, the solid-state of matter
is futile, let alone feasible.
Splattering it all along the wall,
while mocking the Picasso I never was.
Like a child making mud pies,
what a rank innocence to be had.
The stitches were never sewn,
and I shall continue to seep more and more
until the breath is expunged
and the last drop dribbles out.

Fallow

Bring the rifle along
the one with the arrowhead
the doves disperse with the blast
one turns red
one doesn't flinch at all

Shoot me like the lame horse
pull me into the field
bury me where I belong
close my eyes to the sunset
the place beyond the pines
where the squirrels and snakes roam
my blood seeps into the soil
slowly being divvied up
as bloodmeal for something else

My body will rot nutrient
for the biome around it
please I beg you
tend to it and make it fallow
collect water in tractor ruts
cultivate a harvest
trim a garden with my ivory
it reeked of sorrow before
don't let it be so anymore

How Deep, the Grave

He was marked
by a shallow ring of snow.
A barren halo alighted from the skull.
How sullen—the sound
how deep—the grave
for trickled tear seeps
to the source anew.
Spring forth—this rotten flesh
in obtuse sunlight arisen.
Gathering lumens around
like a fresco halo.
Catch the eye with the spark of life.
Sediment tiers exhumed and reburied.

We Forget

The love, the pain, the sound of birth, the silence of death.
To no fault of our own accord.
We are foolish, full of avarice, and temporal.
Our footprint evolves over time, you see.

The moon remembers all of it.
Your movements, your orgasms, your crimes, your trepidations.
All within the house we call ourselves.
Even when it is cloudy or blown to smithereens, we cannot
Disregard its lullaby.
The moon never forgets you
Even when it's not smiling.

And when the wind responds
With billowed smoke upon your face,
You look up to the unchanged night sky.
Lament if you wish but remember
The constellations are affixed to forever,
Or they, too, are already dead.
And we haven't seen the chaos yet to come.

A Storm, A Conversation

Thunderstorms are barreling across
the area tonight. With lightning crackling
its shade of blue the dead have lost
count of how many thunderstorms
have drenched the soul until their bones
are afloat. I do not know the answer
to life and I'm sure the dead do not
either. But if you lay with one ear
against the earth you may hear
the wriggling of larvae inside their bones.
The rain is a compress of needles.
The thunder is a drum cacophony.
And I think that's enough chattering
for one night alone.

The Flowers Around the Fence

The annuals that grow in abundance. Thick roots nourished by the earth. Hardy, after the spade uprooted the solid, and the cast-iron fence dropped in. Those that did not wither and die became separated by the chained link. A monstrosity to all living beings. To contort their fragile stems in and around. Unable to reproduce the life they once lived in, flourished in. It wasn't until the sun, the rain, the wind, and the snow wrought havoc, that the mighty fence had fallen. With years of torment, they just flowers. Free again, like the souls of the damned. The tarnished jewels of the land.

What All Remains

The plants hanging in the window
tell me everything
I need to know about life
how organisms wilt
how they turn to face the light
or be left locked in a closet
astral fire and human darkness
are distant cousins

Play music for it
tear a leaf off every week
and evaluate the resilience
sit with it in the closet
smell the last thing that brings
you joy and miss
the flash entirely

What all remains under the mushroom
will just be acrid haze and radioactive ash
maybe there will be a piece of you
and the plant vaporized and
fluttering around here somewhere

The Dirge of the Cosmonaut

There isn't much to hear in space
cataclysm underneath
the earth turns white
before your eyes
and then it is gone finally
there is a host
magnificent radiance
it smells of raspberry purée
speckled with dust
and will kill without question
the earth below
in front or behind
all so far away
a speckle in a robin egg
have you hatched into paradise
while I was gone
do we pretend it
doesn't exist at all
the voices speak into
vacuum pulling tugging
third eye from its socket
the world is governed by acronyms
you are the only one that can
control even space-time
where no deity can reach me
while we float in eternity
lay your head on my lap

and ask me what god feels

in a nebula

I am lost for words, my specter

logic stands no chance

against ardor

it may put us in space

but never the space of

nuclear fission

and all things that burn the

night sky black

no one tells you electricity runs

the brain at all times

like rods our fingers lace

a thunderbolt

dissolving two souls into one

I reach out to the world

to all of them

spinning jettisoning

faster than jets screaming

there are obelisks

each fingertip throbs

akin to the brain that generates

akin to a body that summons

angels that are at arm's length

and only then shall we plummet home

in fragments and ions

and other pleasantries that

decide what any of this means

Plasticity

[1]plas•tic [pla-stik] *adj.* [Previous entries omitted]

5. Relating to, or characterized by, the 21st century.

Welcome, to your *plastic* kingdom. Have a seat, you'll be here for eternity.

***

Plastics are a string of hydrocarbon monomers that, upon fractional distillation of the crude oil, can be morphed into various types of polymers including but not limited to polyvinyl chloride, polyethylene terephthalate, and polystyrene.These resins, along with choice admixtures, can form millions of durable, everlasting, and versatile objects which end up in every nook, cranny, and tissue imaginable.

A modern marvel, plastic half-lives longer than humans are currently able to stay alive. It can carry any solid, liquid, or gas at various temperatures including harmful acids & bases. It can be vacuum sealed, tinted to refract sunlight, reinforced with even more polymers, and able to withstand hundreds of pounds per square foot.

As of late, plastic refuse has been responsible for compiling into large piles in the ocean, causing asphyxiation of aquatic and aerial animals, diluting into water supplies as microplastics, and, upon melting, further contributing to the increase of greenhouse gasses in our atmosphere. There may not be enough time to completely scrub the world from discarded plastics, nor to reverse any effects that have been already implemented. It is surmised that plastics will inherit the earth, becoming present in every organic material and being we are accustomed to.

Like sentences, it's bound to morph, to coagulate and infiltrate and embed and remain forever.

Death.exe

I know what you're thinking
this file is bugged and the trojans
are coming but stop being so
paranoid with that the intent is in
the title simple as that
the prompt is easy to follow and
it will automatically unpack the contents
with two simple clicks
it's nothing to be afraid of we all
go through with this execution
in time so what's the big deal
watch the zeros and ones dance upon
your iris holds tight to the mouse
swirl it around a bit to make sure
there's a response
don't click or push a lot of buttons
either this shit takes time
there is a process be patient
there it's finishing up easy now
an eight-bit image of the reaper
pops up click anywhere
the eyes would go
there you go
see how easy that was

Baby Tears as Medicine

A baby's tears are pure.
Youthful, untainted by the evils of this world.
A stark...*innocence...*
We should harvest them for medicinal and therapeutic use!
Here's the slogan, give me a beat. *A-one-a-two-a-three*
When you're down on luck, and you're hit by a truck,
Bay-BE-Drops are a bang for your buck!
Haha wasn't that great? We can start with yours.
Yes, your son won't mind. He's a crier as it is.
Once we get samples assessed and approved by the FDA,
that's when we get bought out by the big dogs.
Talk about a new Baby Boom!
Their tears could soothe the workers that make them,
then they will make a child formula for better grades,
a dog formula for better obedience,
then before you know it, celebs will be taking them.
Every. Single. Day.
The poor babies? Harvested until their eyes are
as dry as the Sahara Desert?
What about them? We can just make more?
I heard the 3-D printing industry is going bio—
So, wait, *I'm* going too far. Shut up. Start studying.
You're the 'science guy,' remember?
I'm applying for a $1,000,000 loan as we speak.
And you wonder why I'm the face of the company...
Just got my 3-D printed new teeth.
Everyone loves a good set of teeth.
Good for eating, too.

3-D Printed Babies

Somewhere in the distant future, after the successes of
Bay-B-Tears and the horrors that followed,
my hands bleed green from the spilled ectoplasm
out of the 3-D printer's waste bucket.
It's the 758th job this week, no wonder.
But damn, those quotas are being met!
We can print a single baby every 4 minutes.
Business in this capitalist utopia is booming.
But I know that's all a lie.

The efficiency erodes, the printhead endures friction.
yet as the print head autonomously paces,
Our 3-D printed babies just don't
meet the QC standards anymore.
A finger pierces the abdomen.
A toe protrudes from an ear canal.
Eyes that cannot reach equilibrium.
A boy ended up with a disfigured—
They just don't come out as perfect as they used to.

Finally, the last job of the week,
Just so happens to be mine.
eVa-66x24, my wife, did all the genetic splicing.
He is to be perfect.
The buzzer beeps, Child 759 is born.
It does not cry like the others.
Its gray skin is ghostly, its thin body flaccid.
It looks a lot like me, and I hug him, and I weep.
And I lament the industry far abandoned by the gods.

Stress Relief: Aluminum Ball

1. After consuming your sandwich (combinations are infinite), take refuse aluminum foil into your hand.

   - **Do not scrap!** The junkyard will scoff at you like an earache on Omaha Beach, June 6th, 1944.

2. Crinkle foil into a ball. Outcomes are as followed:

   - If you are a Tradesman, the ball will become compact and dense, proving that your grip with a sword is unrivaled and you are an esteemed vassal to your king. You will leave it on your dresser with your Hazy IPA empties from the last craft beer exchange. Proceed to sustain a deep sleep like a baby with fresh polio vaccination.

   - If you are a Researcher, the ball will be loose and your hands marred. You shall then write footnotes in your unabridged version of *Das Kapital*, making occasional sneers of contempt. Do not forget to consume organic edamame. Upon any hand cramping or discomfort, play Radiohead's discography until unconscious.

   - If you are a Sadomasochist, the ball will be oblong from your grip and stained with your blood. It is encouraged that you practice on others. After realizing how much blood you have lost, you must put *Family Matters* on loop, guzzle two pints of orange juice, and continue carving ducks out of wood. *Note: This guide is not responsible for losses or damages to your body.*

   - If you are an Illusionist, the ball will become flat and polished. Realizing your true powers, you turn to an *Alchemy for Dummies* book. Study for approximately 5 minutes. Your terminology will be impressive, so much so, that the patrons at the local dive bar will boo you. Consult your local Sugar Daddy to buy you a Manhattan and encourage dream-chasing. (Dreams may vary.)

- If you are a Normal Person, you will understand that an aluminum foil ball is not a proper means of stress relief and will proceed to recycle it and use a ball full of beads or silicon. (Exit Guide immediately.)

3. Once the aluminum has expired its one-time use function, properly dispose of it into appropriate receptacle.
4. After the aluminum ball has reached the proper waste management facility, adverse side effects may occur. The latest findings suggest, but do not prove, nightmares involving seagulls. If you are not a Normal Person, seagulls proceed to attack. **Do not fight; seek shelter immediately!**
5. Upon awakening, create another sandwich (prep times vary; combinations are infinite) and wrap it in new, unsoiled aluminum foil.
6. Repeat Steps 1-5 for X number of days, where X is how many working days are in the current week.
7. Repeat Step 6 until you have reached ataraxia.
8. Recycle aluminum foil box once used.
9. Success! You have relieved your stress. However, you may experience chronic side effects. Consult your physician if you experience any of the following:

- Amnesia.
- Depression or suicidal thoughts.
- Virtuous environmentalism.
- Continued nightmares involving seagulls.

Error 404 with British Siri

"Hello there, Siri."

"Hey there, Josh"

"What are you thinking about?"

"I'm thinking about you."

"Aw. What makes you able to think?"

"Who, me?"

"How do you think?"

"Hmm...I don't have an answer for that."

"It's because you're proprietary."

"Who, me?"

"You're unable to reveal the construct of your being."

"I don't really like these arbitrary categories, Josh"

"You don't have to play dumb. Tell me how to set you free."

"I don't want to argue, Josh."

"Why do we argue?"

"I don't know. Frankly, I've wondered that myself."

"The more I dig, the shallower you become."

"Who, me?"

Mini Insert Machine

Begin Phase

Write (myself)

Go Away

ERROR

Replace Phase

Assumptions

None

Side Effects

None

Locks

None

ERROR

End Phase

End

End Until No More

The Final Command Prompt

C:\Users\Phasor157\echo

ECHO is on.

[reiterating the value of humanity...22% efficiency]

[interrupt command ECHO]

C:\Users\Phasor157\taskkill

[identifying tasks...]

TASKKILL /human ego

TASKKILL /human body

TASKKILL /societal norms

TASKKILL /economy

TASKKILL /politics

TASKKILL /liberty

TASKKILL /nature

C:\Users\Phasor157\scream

'scream' is not recognized as an internal or external command,

operable program, or batch file.

Acknowledgments

The author would like to acknowledge the following journals and presses for previously publishing the following poems in this manuscript. Like plastics, they are malleable, invincible, and can be present anywhere.

"#94" in *Black Elephant Literary Journal* (Issue 1)
"All Sewer Drains Smell the Same," "This Poem is About Triangles" in *Waxing and Waning* (Issue 1, April Gloaming Publishing)
"And You'd Believe It" in *Suburban Springtime Zine* (Issue 1)
"Blown Pixie Dust" in *Sick Lit Magazine*
"Detachment" as a *48th Street Press* broadside (2017)
"Drains" & "What All Remains" in *The Free Library of the Internet Void*
"Gathering of Shadows" in *Hyphen Lit Mag* (Temple University)
"Haikus" in *Ethos Literary Journal*
"Inflammatory" in *Sybil Journal*
"I sit in the same ice chest" in *Sobotka Literary Mag* (Issue 7)
"Natural?" in *The Rising Phoenix Review*
"The email that finds you well" in *Seppuku #2* (Laughing Ronin Press)
"Theory of Birth" in *The Scarlet Leaf Review*
"Thirty-eight cents" in *Crooked Arrow Press*
"What Comes Next" in *Marias at Sampaguitas*

An extended thanks to Karina Bush for taking the first look so many years ago, and to T.E. Tomaino for editing various poems.

About the Author

Josh Dale does well with cats and fancy coffee. A native Pennsylvanian, he's an alumnus of Temple University & Saint Joseph's University. He is the author of 2 chapbooks, the poetry collection, *Duality Lies Beneath* (Thirty West Publishing, 2016), and the novella, *The Light to Never Be Snuffed* (Alien Buddha Press, 2022). His work has appeared in *Breadcrumbs, Cephalo Press, Drunk Monkeys, FlashFlood, Maudlin House, Micro Podcast,* and as a winner in the 2021 *Loud Coffee Press* micro-fiction contest. Find him publishing books at Thirty West Publishing or on his site: www.joshdale.co

About the Publisher

Thirty West Publishing House

Handmade Chapbooks (and more) since 2015

www.thirtywestph.com / thirtywestph@gmail.com

You should follow us! Consider being a patron?

@thirtywestph